# BOOK 2: DUMPSTER DIVERS

# Alissa

## and Her clever Dog,

# "Cyber"

## written by Mathew conger
## Illustrated by Dennis Davide

Print information available on the last page

Rev. date: 05/16/2019

To order additional copies of this book, contact:
Xlibris
1-888-795-4274
www.Xlibris.com
Orders@Xlibris.com

BOOK 2: DUMPSTER DIVERS

# Alissa

## AND HER CLEVER DOG,

# "Cyber"

Alissa and her little sister Aubrey decided to take the trash out in order to help their parents clean the house. As soon as they stepped outside of the house, Cyber started barking. "What are you barking at Cyber?" asked Alissa.

Cyber was barking because he didn't like seeing the boys inside the dumpster. Alissa knew something wasn't right. "Drop your trash Aubrey, let's go back inside." said Alissa.

TAP
TAP
TAP

Alissa recognized the two boys from the neighborhood and decided to call the Kids Cyber Response Team. "I'm going to report those two guys because I think they may be up to no good." said Alissa.

"Kids Cyber Response Team, how may I help you?" asked TRON000. "I see two boys that are being suspicious by reading people's trash that has been dumped in a huge trash bin!" exclaimed Alissa. "What could they be up to?" asked Alissa. "Those could be dumpster divers!" yelled TRON000. Dumpster divers like to search for trash containing important information such as passwords, social security numbers, and credit card numbers. "Make sure you shred all of your trash and never write down your passwords on paper or yellow stickies." said TRON000.

SHRED-O-MATIC

10

"Thanks for your suggestions TRON000!" yelled Alissa. "Now we feel safe from giving our important information to those dumpster divers." said Alissa.

Alissa and Aubrey returned to the dumpster with their trash. "Now we don't have to worry about anyone finding important information inside our trash." said Alissa.

The two dumpster divers were not happy to see that Alissa and Aubrey's trash bags were full of shred.

"Who's a good doggy?" asked Aubrey. "That's right!" said Alissa. Alissa and Aubrey gave Cyber a snack because Cyber alerted them when he noticed the two boys being suspicious dumpster divers.

"I doubt those guys will come back since we shred all of our trash now!" shouted Alissa.

**The end.**

Printed in the United States
By Bookmasters